READ & RESPOND

Bringing the best books to life in the classroom

Activities based on
The Boy in the Striped Pyjamas
By John Boyne

Terms and conditions

IMPORTANT – PERMITTED USE AND WARNINGS – READ CAREFULLY BEFORE USING

IF YOU ACCEPT THE ABOVE CONDITIONS YOU MAY PROCEED TO USE THE CD-ROM.

Recommended system requirements:
Windows: XP (Service Pack 3), Vista (Service Pack 2), Windows 7 or Windows 8 with 2.33GHz processor
Mac: OS 10.6 to 10.8 with Intel Core™ Duo processor
1GB RAM (recommended)
1024 x 768 Screen resolution
CD-ROM drive (24x speed recommended)
Adobe Reader (version 9 recommended for Mac users)
Broadband internet connections (for installation and updates)

For all technical support queries (including no CD drive), please phone Scholastic Customer Services on 0845 6039091.

Designed using Adobe Indesign
Scholastic Education, an imprint of Scholastic Ltd
Book End, Range Road, Witney, Oxfordshire, OX29 0YD
Registered office: Westfield Road, Southam,
Warwickshire CV47 0RA

Printed and bound by Ashford Colour Press
© 2017 Scholastic Ltd
1 2 3 4 5 6 7 8 9 7 8 9 0 1 2 3 4 5 6

British Library Cataloguing-in-Publication Data
A catalogue record for this book is available from the British Library.
ISBN 978-1407-16071-9

Author Helen Lewis
Editorial team Rachel Morgan, Jenny Wilcox, Catherine Allison, Vicky Butt
Series designer Neil Salt
Designer Anna Oliwa
Illustrator Natalie Ortega/Beehive illustration
Digital development Hannah Barnett, Phil Crothers and MWA Technologies Private Ltd
Photograph Mother Teresa of Calcutta, India: © Tim Graham & robertharding/superstock.com

Acknowledgements
The publishers gratefully acknowledge permission to reproduce the following copyright material:
Penguin Random House UK for the use of the cover and extract text from *The Boy in the Striped Pyjamas* written by John Boyne, first published in Great Britain by David Fickling Books, (when an imprint of Random House Children's Publishers UK A Penguin Random House Company) Text copyright © John Boyne, 2006. (2016, Definitions Books)

Every effort has been made to trace copyright holders for the works reproduced in this book, and the publishers apologise for any inadvertent omissions.

CONTENTS ▼

INTRODUCTION

Read & Respond provides teaching ideas related to a specific children's book. The series focuses on best-loved books and brings you ways to use them to engage your class and enthuse the children about reading.

The book is divided into different sections:

- **About the book and author:** gives you some background information about the book and the author.

- **Guided reading:** breaks the book down into sections and gives notes for using it with guided reading groups. A bookmark has been provided on page 12 containing comprehension questions. The children can be directed to refer to these as they read.

- **Shared reading:** provides extracts from the children's books with associated notes for focused work. There is also one non-fiction extract that relates to the children's book.

- **Grammar, punctuation & spelling:** provides word-level work related to the children's book so you can teach grammar, punctuation and spelling in context.

- **Plot, character & setting:** contains activity ideas focused on the plot, characters and the setting of the story.

- **Talk about it:** has speaking and listening activities related to the children's book. These activities may be based directly on the children's book or be broadly based on the themes and concepts of the story.

- **Get writing:** provides writing activities related to the children's book. These activities may be based directly on the children's book or be broadly based on the themes and concepts of the story.

- **Assessment:** contains short activities that will help you assess whether the children have understood concepts and curriculum objectives. They are designed to be informal activities to feed into your planning.

The activities follow the same format:

- **Objective:** the objective for the lesson. It will be based upon a curriculum objective, but will often be more specific to the focus being covered.

- **What you need:** a list of resources you need to teach the lesson, including digital resources (printable pages, interactive activities and media resources, see page 5).

- **What to do:** the activity notes.

- **Differentiation:** this is provided where specific and useful differentiation advice can be given to support and/or extend the learning in the activity. Differentiation by providing additional adult support has not been included as this will be at a teacher's discretion based upon specific children's needs and ability, as well as the availability of support.

The activities are numbered for reference within each section and should move through the text sequentially – so you can use the lesson while you are reading the book. Once you have read the book, most of the activities can be used in any order you wish.

Below are brief guidance notes for using the CD-ROM. For more detailed information, please click on the '?' button in the top right-hand corner of the screen.

The program contains the following:
- the extract pages from the book
- all of the photocopiable pages from the book
- additional printable pages
- interactive on-screen activities
- media resources.

Getting started

Put the CD-ROM into your CD-ROM drive. If you do not have a CD-ROM drive, phone Scholastic Customer Services on 0845 6039091.

- For Windows users, the install wizard should autorun, if it fails to do so then navigate to your CD-ROM drive. Then follow the installation process.
- For Mac users, copy the disk image file to your hard drive. After it has finished copying double click it to mount the disk image. Navigate to the mounted disk image and run the installer. After installation the disk image can be unmounted and the DMG can be deleted from the hard drive.
- To install on a network, see the ReadMe file located on the CD-ROM (navigate to your drive).

To complete the installation of the program, you need to open the program and click 'Update' in the pop-up. Please note – this CD-ROM is web-enabled and the content will be downloaded from the internet to your hard drive to populate the CD-ROM with the relevant resources. This only needs to be done on first use. After this you will be able to use the CD-ROM without an internet connection. If at any point any content is updated, you will receive another pop-up upon start up when there is an internet connection.

Main menu

The Main menu is the first screen that appears. Here you can access: terms and conditions, registration links, how to use the CD-ROM and credits. To access a specific book, click on the relevant button (Note only titles installed will be available). You can filter by the

drop-down lists if you wish. You can search all resources by clicking 'Search' in the bottom left-hand corner. You can also log in and access favourites that you have bookmarked.

Resources

By clicking on a book on the main menu, you are taken to the resources for that title. The resources are: Media, Interactives, Extracts and Printables. Select the category and then launch a resource by clicking the 'Play' button.

Teacher settings

In the top right-hand corner of the screen is a small 'T' button. This is the teacher settings area. It is password protected, the password is: login. This area will allow you to choose the print quality settings for interactive activities ('Default' or 'Best') and also allow you to check for updates to the program or re-download all content to the disk via 'Refresh all content'. You can also set up user logins so that you can save and access favourites. Once a user is set up, they can enter by clicking the login link underneath the 'T' and '?' buttons.

Search

You can access an all resources search by clicking the 'Search' button on the bottom left of the Main menu. You can search for activities by type (using the drop-down filter) or by keyword by typing into the box. You can then assign resources to your favourites area or launch them directly from the search area.

CURRICULUM LINKS

Section	Activity	Curriculum objectives
Guided reading		Comprehension: To maintain positive attitudes to reading and understanding of what they read.
Shared reading	1	Comprehension: To identify and discuss themes and conventions in and across a wide range of writing.
	2	Comprehension: To draw inferences such as inferring characters' feelings, thoughts and motives from their actions, and to justify inferences with evidence.
	3	Comprehension: To discuss and evaluate how authors use language, including figurative language, and to consider the impact on the reader.
	4	Comprehension: To check that the book makes sense to them, discussing their understanding and explore the meaning of words in context.
Grammar, punctuation & spelling	1	Composition: To use expanded noun phrases to convey complicated information concisely.
	2	Composition: To use a wide range of devices to build cohesion within and across paragraphs.
	3	Transcription: To use further prefixes and suffixes and understand the guidance for adding them.
	4	Transcription: To use a thesaurus.
	5	Composition: To use brackets, dashes or commas to indicate parenthesis.
	6	Transcription: To spell some words with 'silent' letters.
Plot, character & setting	1	Composition: To précis longer passages.
	2	Comprehension: To draw inferences such as inferring characters' feelings, thoughts and motives from their actions, and to justify inferences with evidence.
	3	Comprehension: To identify how language, structure and presentation contribute to meaning.
	4	Comprehension: To draw inferences such as inferring characters' feelings, thoughts and motives from their actions, and to justify inferences with evidence.
	5	Comprehension: To make comparisons within and across books.
	6	Comprehension: To identify and discuss themes and conventions in and across a wide range of writing.
	7	Comprehension: To identify and discuss themes and conventions in and across a wide range of writing.
	8	Comprehension: To discuss and evaluate how authors use language, including figurative language, considering the impact on the reader.

Section	Activity	Curriculum objectives
Talk about it	1	Spoken language: To give well-structured descriptions, explanations and narratives for different purposes, including for expressing feelings.
	2	Spoken language: To participate in discussions, presentations, performances, role play, improvisations and debates.
	3	Spoken language: To participate in discussions, presentations, performances, role play, improvisations and debates.
	4	Spoken language: To give well-structured descriptions and explanations for different purposes, including for expressing feelings.
	5	Spoken language: To articulate and justify answers, arguments and opinions.
	6	Spoken language: To participate in discussions, presentations, performances, role play, improvisations and debates.
Get writing	1	Composition: To select appropriate grammar and vocabulary, understanding how such choices can change and enhance meaning.
	2	Composition: To identify the audience for and purpose of the writing, selecting the appropriate form and using other similar writing as models for their own.
	3	Composition: To note and develop initial ideas, drawing on reading and research where necessary.
	4	Composition: To describe settings, characters and atmosphere and integrate dialogue to convey character and advance the action.
	5	Composition: To assess the effectiveness of their own and others' writing.
	6	Composition: To perform own compositions, using appropriate intonation, volume, and movement so that meaning is clear.
Assessment	1	Comprehension: To draw inferences such as inferring characters' feelings, thoughts and motives from their actions, and to justify inferences with evidence.
	2	Comprehension: To participate in discussions about books that are read to them and those they can read for themselves, building on their own and others' ideas and challenging views courteously.
	3	Comprehension: To ask questions to improve their understanding of a text.
	4	Comprehension: To recommend books that they have read to their peers, giving reasons for their choices.
	5	Composition: To propose changes to vocabulary, grammar and punctuation to enhance effects and clarify meaning.
	6	Comprehension: To explain and discuss their understanding of what they have read, including through formal presentations and debates, maintaining a focus on the topic and using notes where necessary.

THE BOY IN THE STRIPED PYJAMAS

About the book

When nine-year-old Bruno returns home from school one day, he discovers that his belongings are being packed in crates. His father has received a promotion and the family must move to a new house far, far away, where there is no one for him to play with and nothing to do. A tall fence stretches as far as the eye can see and cuts him off from the strange people in the distance.

But Bruno longs to be an explorer and decides that there must be more to this desolate new place than meets the eye. While exploring his new environment, he meets another boy whose life and circumstances are very different from his own, and their meeting results in a friendship that has devastating consequences.

The Boy in the Striped Pyjamas has won two Irish Book Awards, topped the *New York Times* bestseller list, and was adapted into a Miramax feature film. It has sold more than six million copies worldwide.

About the author

John Boyne was born in Ireland in 1971, and studied English Literature at Trinity College, Dublin. He went on to take an MA in Creative Writing at the University of East Anglia, Norwich, and he now offers a scholarship to Irish students enrolled on the same course.

To date, John Boyne has published nine novels for adults and five for younger readers, including *Noah Barleywater Runs Away* and *The Terrible Thing That Happened to Barnaby Brocket*. His books have been published in 48 languages.

John Boyne is a regular book reviewer for the *Irish Times* and has been a judge for both the Hennessy Literary Awards and the International IMPAC Dublin Literary Award, as well as chairing the jury for the 2015 Scotiabank Giller Prize.

In 2012, John Boyne was awarded the Hennessy Literary 'Hall of Fame' Award for his body of work. He has also won three Irish Book Awards, for Children's Book of the Year, People's Choice Book of the Year and Short Story of the Year. He has won a number of international literary awards, including the Gustav Heinemann Peace Prize in Germany. In 2015, he was awarded an Honorary Doctorate of Letters from the University of East Anglia.

Key facts

The Boy in the Striped Pyjamas

Author: John Boyne

First published: 2006

Awards: Irish Book Award Children's Book of the Year, Irish Book Award People's Choice Book of the Year, Bisto Book of the Year, Qué Leer Award Best International Novel of the Year (Spain), Orange Prize Readers Group Book of the Year.

Did you know? The story started as an idea John Boyne had of two boys talking at a fence. Four days later, he had completed the first draft of the novel!

Cover story

Before you begin reading the story, look at the front cover of the book with the class. Ask: *What can you tell about the story just by looking at the front cover?* Establish the fact that the front cover gives away nothing about the story.

Turn over the book and read the blurb on the back cover. Ask: *Does the blurb give you any more information?* (It says the story is difficult to describe, and that it's about a nine-year-old boy called Bruno who goes on a journey that ends up at a fence.) *Which techniques are used in the blurb to encourage potential readers to buy the book?* (The blurb continues the sense of mystery generated by the front cover, which is designed to pique the reader's curiosity; it also includes newspaper reviews implying that the story is powerful. They say the story has a 'killer punch', and that it 'lingers in the mind'.)

Ask: *Is it usual for the cover of a book to give away so little of the story?* (no) *Why do you think this book is different?* (A mystery about what is really happening might be an important part of the story.) Open the book to the title page. Get children to compare the title page with the front cover. Ask: *What appears on the title page that does not appear on the front cover?* (the words 'a fable by') Ask: *What is a fable?* (A story that features animals or other non-human characters that are given human qualities, and that gives a particular moral lesson.) *Given that the author describes the book as a fable, what features do you think the story might have?*

Leaving home

Read the first chapter together. Organise the children into pairs to discuss (and possibly make notes on) question 1 from the Guided Reading bookmark (page 12). Ask a volunteer to share their summary with the class.

Ask: *What do you learn about Bruno from the first chapter?* (He lives with his mother, father and sister, doesn't get on with his sister, he doesn't know what job his father does, he lives in Berlin, he goes to school, he has friends called Karl, Martin and Daniel, he says what he thinks, he lives in a big house, he enjoys sliding down the banister, and he loves his grandparents.)
Together, discuss question 2 from the bookmark.

Life at Out-With

Read Chapters 2 to 5 together.

After reading Chapters 2 and 3, ask: *In what ways is life at Out-With different from life in Berlin? How does Bruno feel about his sister? How do you know? Why does he feel this way?*

After reading Chapter 4, ask children to describe in their own words what Gretel and Bruno saw through the window. You could ask them to draw a labelled plan drawing of Out-With.

After reading Chapter 5, ask: *What is the same about the two trains at the station? What is different about them? What do you think is going on? What aspects of Bruno's character are revealed in Chapter 5?* Encourage children to explain their answers with evidence from the text.

Discuss questions 3 and 9 from the bookmark.

Homesickness

Read Chapters 6 to 9 together.

After reading Chapter 6, ask: *Why do you think Maria is reluctant to tell Bruno what she thinks?* (She is worried that what she says might get back to Bruno's father.) *What does this suggest?* (Maria is scared of Bruno's father.) *What other evidence is there that Maria is scared of Bruno's father?* (She begs him not to voice his opinion about his father's decision.) *What aspect of Bruno's father is revealed when Maria tells Bruno about how she came to live with them?* (He is capable of being kind.)

After reading Chapter 7, ask: *Why did Bruno decide to make the tyre swing? What do you learn about Lieutenant Kotler in this chapter? What do you learn about Pavel?* When Bruno asks Pavel how long he's been at Out-With he replies 'I think I've always been here.' Ask: *What do you think Pavel means by this?* Draw children's attention to the final three paragraphs of Chapter 7. Ask: *What does Bruno hear his mother saying to Pavel? What does Bruno think his mother's motivation is for saying this? What do you think her real motivation is?*

After reading Chapter 9, ask: *In what ways does Bruno misunderstand Herr Liszt? What do you think Herr Liszt really means when he talks about 'the Fatherland'* (Germany) *and 'the wrongs that have been done to you'?* (The reparations Germany was forced to make at the end of the First World War, which included losing territory, and paying financial compensation to countries damaged during the war.) *Why does Bruno start exploring outdoors, even though his parents have told him it is not allowed? What do you think might happen next? Explain your thinking, based on what has already happened in the story.*

Discuss questions 10, 11 and 12 from the bookmark.

....

Friendship and betrayal

Read Chapters 10 to 15 together.

After reading Chapter 10, ask: *What similarities are there between Shmuel and Bruno? What differences are there between the two boys? What is the significance of these differences?*

After reading Chapter 11, ask: *Who do you think The Fury is? What do you find out about him from this chapter? Why do you think the author includes this chapter in the story?*

After reading Chapter 12, ask: *How did Shmuel come to be behind the fence? In what ways does Bruno relate Shmuel's story back to himself? What does this tell you about Bruno?*

After reading Chapter 13, ask: *Why do you think Bruno's father asks Lieutenant Kotler so many questions about his own father?* (He suspects Kotler's father may not be a Nazi sympathiser.) *What further evidence is there in this chapter of Lieutenant Kotler's cruelty? Why do you think the author does not describe what Kotler did to Pavel?*

After reading Chapter 14, ask: *What clues are there in this chapter that Bruno doesn't have any idea about what's going on on the other side of the fence? What lie does Bruno tell? Why do you think he tells it?*

After reading Chapter 15, ask: *How does the first half of the chapter contrast with the second half of the chapter?* (The first half is light and humorous; the second half is tense and frightening.) Ask: *Why do you think the author made the first half of the chapter light and humorous?* (To emphasise the fear and tension in the second half.) Ask: *Do you think Bruno meant to betray Shmuel? Why do you think he did it?* (He was afraid of what Lieutenant Kotler would do to him if he admitted to being Shmuel's friend.)

Discuss questions 6, 7 and 8 from the bookmark.

....

Changes

Read Chapters 16 to 18 together.

Ask children to discuss (and maybe make a list of) all the changes that take place in these three chapters. (Grandmother dies; Kotler is transferred; Gretel replaces her dolls with maps of Europe; Bruno has his head shaved; Father decides to send the family back to Berlin; Shmuel's father has gone missing.)

Ask questions about the changes, for example: *Why do you think Kotler is transferred? What is the* significance of Gretel replacing her dolls with maps of Europe? What part does Bruno play in his father's decision to send the family back to Berlin? What do you think has happened to Shmuel's father?

Ask: *What is the effect of so many changes taking place in such a short time?* (It feels like the story is accelerating; that events are gathering pace and rushing towards the conclusion.)

Draw children's attention to the fact that in Chapter 18 Shmuel lifts up the fence enough to allow a small boy to fit underneath. Ask: *What reasons do you think Shmuel has for not crawling under the fence himself? What reasons do you think the author has for Shmuel not crawling under the fence?*

Discuss question 4 from the bookmark.

The end

Read Chapters 19 and 20 together.

After reading Chapter 19, ask: *What do you think happened to Bruno and Shmuel? Why do you think the author only hints at what happened rather than spelling it out? What devices does the author use to create tension and anticipation in this chapter?* (He gives clues that something bad is going to happen – the way the people in the camp are behaving, the loud noises 'like gunshots', and Shmuel's statement that he never sees anyone after they've gone on a march. Bruno also gets several chances to escape, which increases the tension even further: the rain in the morning means Bruno may have to call off the plan, and once he's gone over the fence, he announces twice that he's going to leave, but the first time he changes his mind and the second time he doesn't get the chance.

After reading Chapter 20, ask: *Which family member do you think suffered the most over Bruno's disappearance? Explain your thinking. What do you think happened to Father when the soldiers came for him? Why do you think this? What is the significance of the last three sentences of the book?*

Discuss questions 15 and 16 from the bookmark.

Second reading

Use a second reading of the novel to explore key features of the story in more depth. Discuss questions 5, 13 and 14 from the bookmark.

SCHOLASTIC READ & RESPOND
Bringing the best books to life in the classroom

The Boy in the Striped Pyjamas
by John Boyne

Focus on…
Meaning

1. Summarise the first chapter.

2. What themes does the first chapter introduce? How do you think they might be explored in the rest of the book?

3. What clues have you found in what you have read so far about what's really going on? What do the clues suggest?

4. Predict what might happen next. Justify your answer by giving evidence from what you have read so far.

5. Who do you think is the boy referred to in the book title? Explain your thinking.

Focus on…
Organisation

6. How do the chapter titles add to the story?

7. Suggest an alternative title for a chapter you have read.

8. The story is mainly told in chronological order, but the author uses flashbacks in Chapters 5, 8 and 11. Why do you think the author does this?

SCHOLASTIC READ & RESPOND
Bringing the best books to life in the classroom

The Boy in the Striped Pyjamas
by John Boyne

Focus on…
Language and features

9. Find an example of repeated sentences or phrases. Why do you think the author uses repetition?

10. What devices does the author use to build tension and anticipation?

11. This book is a serious story that uses humour. How does humour add to the story?

12. What devices does the author use to create humour?

Focus on…
Purpose, viewpoints and effects

13. Why do you think the author tells the story from Bruno's point of view rather than from Shmuel's?

14. In what ways do the boys benefit from their friendship with each other?

15. Which part of the story do you find the most memorable? Explain your reasons.

16. The author describes this book as a fable – a story with a moral. What do you think is the moral at the heart of the story?

Extract 1

- Display an enlarged copy of Extract 1 (from Chapter 4) and read it aloud together. You could ask individual children to read the parts of Bruno and Gretel.

- Ask: *How does this extract show the difference between Gretel's character and Bruno's character?* (through their different attitudes to the children on the other side of the fence) Ask: *What does each child's attitude towards the children on the other side of the fence tell you about their character?* (Gretel judges other people; she shows this through her unsympathetic attitude towards the children, criticising them for being dirty. Bruno tries to understand other people. He shows this by suggesting reasons why the children might be dirty.)

- Revise the term 'theme' – what a story is about at the deepest level. Remind children that themes can often be expressed by a single word – usually an abstract noun, such as friendship. Establish that there are several themes that run through the novel, and that some of them are explored in this extract. Ask: *What themes are explored in this extract?* Give children time to discuss this question with a partner.

- Get back together as a class to share ideas. Themes explored in this extract include innocence/misunderstanding, otherness, brutality and wilful blindness. Ask children to back up their suggestions of themes with evidence from the text.

- Pick one of the themes children have identified. Ask: *How has this theme been explored in what you have read of the book so far? How do you think it might be developed in the rest of the book?*

Extract 2

- Display an enlarged copy of Extract 2 (from Chapter 15) and read it aloud together. Ask: *How do the boys show their fear?* (Shmuel is unable to speak, his eyes plead for help, and tears well up in his eyes; Bruno can't remember how to say 'yes' and he stammers.)

- Ask: *What do you think the boys are afraid of?* Use evidence from the text to support your answer. (They are afraid that Lieutenant Kotler might beat them – or worse. The text says 'all Bruno could think of was the afternoon when he had seen him shooting a dog and the evening when Pavel had made him so angry that he–'.)

- Ask: *How do you think Lieutenant Kotler is feeling?* (angry) Ask children to underline parts of the text that imply this (for example, …shouted Lieutenant Kotler, …in a louder voice, …he was advancing on him now, …his face growing red, …'I won't ask you a third time').

- Ask: *Why is Lieutenant Kotler angry with Shmuel?* (He thinks Shmuel has stolen food from the fridge.) *Why is he angry with Bruno?* (He thinks Bruno has been talking to the prisoners.) Ask: *Why do you think Bruno talking to the prisoners would make Lieutenant Kotler angry?*

- Ask: *Do you think Bruno means to betray Shmuel?* (no) *Explain your answer with reference to the text.* (Firstly he tries to answer yes to Kotler's question, but can't; then he tries to avoid answering the question altogether; it is only when Kotler comes towards him and Bruno remembers instances of his cruelty that he answers no.)

Extract 3

- Display an enlarged copy of Extract 3 (from Chapter 18) and read it aloud together. You could ask individual children to read the parts of Bruno and Shmuel.

- Ask: *What gives Bruno his brainwave?* (The fact that he looks like Shmuel since he had his head shaved.) *What motivates Bruno to carry out the plan?* (He wants to do some exploring.) *What is the most important aspect of the plan for Shmuel?* (That Bruno will be able to help him look for his father.)

- Ask: *What does Bruno call the uniform worn by the people behind the fence?* (striped pyjamas) *What is the effect on the reader of Bruno using this name for the uniform?* (It makes the reader uncomfortable because it shows that Bruno has no idea what is going on; it suggests he might think the people behind the fence are lounging around and taking it easy, when in fact they are overworked and abused prisoners.)

- Ask: *Why does Bruno say the adventure will be 'Our final adventure'?* (He's due to leave for Berlin the next day.) *What atmosphere do you think the author is trying to create by using the phrase 'our final adventure'?* (He's trying to create tension by hinting that the story might end badly.)

- Organise children into pairs to discuss the following question: *What do you think might happen when Bruno carries out his plan?* Encourage children to explain the reasons for their thinking to their partner.

- Take an informal poll about what children think might happen when Bruno carries out his plan.

Extract 4

- Read together an enlarged copy of Extract 4. Discuss the genre and style of writing and compare it to the previous extracts. Ask: *Is this text fiction or non-fiction? Descriptive or informative? Does it have facts, opinions or both?*

- Number the paragraphs. Ask children to sum up what each paragraph is about; for example, Paragraph 1: What the Holocaust was. Ask children to write a similar précis for each of the remaining paragraphs.

- Ask children to find and underline the word 'Aryan' wherever it appears in the text. Ask: *What do you notice about the way this word is written?* (It's written in inverted commas.) Ask: *Why do you think 'Aryan' is written in inverted commas?* (The author is suggesting that there is really no such thing as the Aryan race.)

- Draw children's attention to the first sentence of Paragraph 2. Ask: *What does the author's choice of the word 'seized' suggest?* (that the Nazis took power by force)

- Ask children to locate and underline the following words: 'persecuted' (paragraph 2), 'appalling' (paragraph 4) and 'liberated' (paragraph 6). Ask: *What other word or phrase could you use to replace each of these words without changing the meaning of the sentence?* Organise children into pairs to discuss ideas.

- Ask pairs to share their ideas with the rest of the class. Suitable synonyms include:
  - persecuted: victimised, oppressed, harassed
  - appalling: dreadful, awful, horrific, terrible
  - liberated: freed, set free, released, rescued

- Display and discuss the media resource 'The liberation of Auschwitz'.

Extract 1

Chapter 4

'Look over there,' said Bruno, and Gretel followed the direction of the finger he was pointing and saw, emerging from a hut in the distance, a group of children huddled together and being shouted at by a group of soldiers. The more they were shouted at, the closer they huddled together, but then one of the soldiers lunged towards them and they separated and seemed to do what he had wanted them to do all along, which was to stand in a single line. When they did, the soldiers all started to laugh and applaud them.

'It must be some sort of rehearsal,' suggested Gretel, ignoring the fact that some of the children, even some of the older ones, even the ones as grown up as her, looked as if they were crying.

'I told you there were children here,' said Bruno.

'Not the type of children I want to play with,' said Gretel in a determined voice. 'They look filthy. Hilda and Isobel and Louise have a bath every morning and so do I. Those children look like they've never had a bath in their lives.'

'It does look very dirty over there,' said Bruno. 'But maybe they don't have any baths?'

'Don't be stupid,' said Gretel, despite the fact that she had been told time and time again that she was not to call her brother stupid. 'What kind of people don't have baths?'

'I don't know,' said Bruno. 'People who don't have any hot water?'

Gretel watched for another few moments before shivering and turning away. 'I'm going back to my room to arrange my dolls,' she said. 'The view is decidedly nicer from there.'

Extract 2

Chapter 15

'You have been eating,' insisted Lieutenant Kotler. 'Did you steal something from that fridge?'

Shmuel opened his mouth and closed it. He opened it again and tried to find words, but there were none. He looked towards Bruno, his eyes pleading for help.

'Answer me!' shouted Lieutenant Kotler. 'Did you steal something from that fridge?'

'No, sir. He gave it to me,' said Shmuel, tears welling up in his eyes as he threw a sideways glance at Bruno. 'He's my friend,' he added.

'Your…?' began Lieutenant Kotler, looking across at Bruno in confusion. He hesitated. 'What do you mean he's your friend?' he asked. 'Do you know this boy, Bruno?'

Bruno's mouth dropped open and he tried to remember the way you used your mouth if you wanted to say the word 'yes'. He'd never seen anyone look so terrified as Shmuel did at that moment and he wanted to say the right thing to make things better, but then he realized that he couldn't; because he was feeling just as terrified himself.

'Do you know this boy?' repeated Kotler in a louder voice. 'Have you been talking to the prisoners?'

'I … he was here when I came in,' said Bruno. 'He was cleaning glasses.'

'That's not what I asked you,' said Kotler. 'Have you seen him before? Have you talked to him? Why does he say you're his friend?'

Bruno wished he could run away. He hated Lieutenant Kotler, but he was advancing on him now and all Bruno could think of was the afternoon when he had seen him shooting a dog and the evening when Pavel had made him so angry that he—

'Tell me, Bruno!' shouted Kotler, his face growing red. 'I won't ask you a third time.'

'I've never spoken to him,' said Bruno immediately. 'I've never seen him before in my life. I don't know him.'

Extract 3

Chapter 18

Neither boy said anything for a moment. Suddenly Bruno had a brainwave.

'Unless …' he began, thinking about it for a moment and allowing a plan to hatch in his head. He reached a hand up to his head and felt where his hair used to be but was now just stubble that hadn't fully grown back. 'Don't you remember that you said I looked like you?' he asked Shmuel. 'Since I had my head shaved?'

'Only fatter,' conceded Shmuel.

'Well, if that's the case,' said Bruno, 'and if I had a pair of striped pyjamas too, then I could come over on a visit and no one would be any the wiser.'

Shmuel's face brightened up and he broke into a wide smile. 'Do you think so?' he asked. 'Would you do it?'

'Of course,' said Bruno. 'It would be a great adventure. Our final adventure. I could do some exploring at last.'

'And you could help me look for Papa,' said Shmuel.

'Why not?' said Bruno. 'We'll take a walk around and see whether we can find any evidence. That's always wise when you're exploring. The only problem is getting a spare pair of striped pyjamas.'

Shmuel shook his head. 'That's all right,' said. 'There's a hut where they keep them. I can get some in my size and bring them with me. Then you can change and we can look for Papa.'

'Wonderful,' said Bruno, caught up in the enthusiasm of the moment. 'Then it's a plan.'

'We'll meet at the same time tomorrow,' said Shmuel.

'Don't be late this time,' said Bruno, standing up and dusting himself down. 'And don't forget the striped pyjamas.'

Extract 4

The Holocaust

The Holocaust was the murder of millions of people by the German state between 1933 and 1945.

In 1933, the Nazi party seized power in Germany. The Nazis were racists. They claimed the Germans belonged to a race called the 'Aryans', who were superior to other people. The Nazis persecuted non-'Aryan' people, as well as anyone who disagreed with their policies. The leader of the Nazi party, Adolf Hitler, hated Jewish people in particular.

Beginning in 1939, the Nazis forced hundreds of thousands of Jews out of their homes and into inner-city slums called ghettoes. The homes and businesses they left behind were given to 'Aryans'. Life in the ghettoes was incredibly hard. Hundreds of people would often be living in an area previously occupied by only a handful of families. Food was scarce, and many people starved to death. The sewers could not cope with the large numbers of people, and medicines were not allowed in, so many people died from disease. Anyone who tried to escape from a ghetto was executed.

The Nazis built enormous prisons called concentration camps, where they sent anyone they didn't like. Conditions in the concentration camps were appalling. Prisoners were starved, and were often tortured or worked to death. Disease was widespread.

In 1942, the Nazis set up six death camps in Poland. They used specially built gas chambers to kill people with poison gas. The largest of these camps was called Auschwitz. Over a million prisoners died at Auschwitz – about ninety percent of them Jewish.

Today, there are many museums and monuments around the world that serve as memorials to the victims of the Holocaust. International Holocaust Remembrance Day is on 27 January every year. This marks the day in 1945 when the surviving prisoners in Auschwitz were liberated by Russian troops.

1. Expanded noun phrases

Objective

To use expanded noun phrases to convey information concisely.

What you need

Copies of *The Boy in the Striped Pyjamas,* photocopiable page 22 'Build a noun phrase', media resource 'Pictures for noun phrases'.

What to do

- Ask children to define the term 'noun' (for example, a person, animal, object, idea or place). Ask: *What is a noun phrase?* (A group of words that contains a noun.) Explain that noun phrases give extra information about the noun, and they can make your writing more interesting to read.

- Display the photos in the media resource 'Pictures for noun phrases' one at a time. For each photo, ask children to suggest a noun to match it (for example, street). Ask children to use the noun in a noun phrase (for example, a winding street) and then expand the noun phrase a couple of times (for example, a narrow, winding street; a narrow, winding street on a hill).

- Give children copies of photocopiable page 22 'Build a noun phrase' to complete, asking them to write an expanded noun phrase to describe each picture (for example, 'a rusty old bike with a bent wheel'). You could ask finishers to produce their own version of the activity to give to a friend.

- Ask children who have done the extension activity to share what they have written with the rest of the class.

Differentiation

Extension: Challenge children to choose a scene from *The Boy in the Striped Pyjamas* that has a strong atmosphere. Get them to identify noun phrases and the adjectives/detail they contain, and note the impact of the description on the overall tone of the scene. Ask children to rewrite the sentences using different adjectives/detail for each noun phrase, in order to create a contrasting atmosphere.

2. Dot, dot, dot...

Objective

To use ellipsis.

What you need

Copies of *The Boy in the Striped Pyjamas,* interactive activity 'Dot, dot, dot…'.

What to do

- Give out sharing copies of *The Boy in the Striped Pyjamas.*

- On the board write an ellipsis (…). Ask: *What is this punctuation mark called?*

- Ask children, working with a partner, to look for instances of ellipses in the novel, and to make notes about the ways in which they are used.

- Ask children to share their observations. Establish through discussion that an ellipsis has two main uses: to show where something is missed out (a word, phrase or sentence), or to mark a pause. Ask children to provide examples of both of these uses in *The Boy in the Striped Pyjamas.* Where an ellipsis is used to denote something has been missed out, ask children to suggest what the missed out word(s) might be.

- Display the interactive activity 'Dot, dot, dot…'. Work through the first screen as a class, ticking the one sentence with correct punctuation. Then give children time to complete the next four screens working in pairs or individually.

- Challenge finishers to make up their own sentences containing ellipses based on the characters in *The Boy in the Striped Pyjamas.*

Differentiation

Support: Pair children up for the interactive activity, matching the less confident learners with a slightly more confident partner.

3. Significant suffixes

Objective

To use the suffixes 'ant', 'ance'/'ancy', 'ent' and 'ence'/'ency'.

What you need

Photocopiable page 23 'Significant suffixes', dictionaries.

What to do

- Ask: *What is a suffix?* (a string of letters used at the end of one word to turn it into another word)

- Write the suffixes 'ant', 'ance'/'ancy' on one side of the board and the suffixes 'ent' and 'ence'/'ency' on the other. Explain that these suffixes are used to form adjectives and nouns from verbs. For example:
  - 'observe' (verb) + 'ant' = 'observant' (adjective)
    'observe' (verb) + 'ance' = 'observance' (noun)
  - 'confide' (verb) + 'ent' = 'confident' (adjective)
    'confide' (verb) + 'ence' = 'confidence' (noun)

- Give out copies of photocopiable page 23 'Significant suffixes'. Read and discuss the rules for adding the suffixes at the top of the page. Use the rules to work through the first two or three questions in the first task.

- Ask children, working in pairs or individually, to complete the photocopiable sheet. (Answers: A 1. assistant, 2. occupant, 3. innocent 4. expectant, 5. intelligent, 6, observant, 7. frequent, 8. decent; Answers B assistance, occupancy, expectancy, intelligence, observance, frequence/frequency, decency)

Differentiation

Support: For the second task on the photocopiable sheet, ask children to write sentences for only one or two of the words.
Extension: Explain that there are many words that do not follow the rules on the photocopiable sheet. Ask children to use a dictionary to find and note examples of these exception words. They can feed these back to the whole class.

4. Better words

Objective

To use a thesaurus.

What you need

Copies of *The Boy in the Striped Pyjamas*, photocopiable page 24 'Better words', thesauruses.

What to do

- Write a sentence containing the word 'sad' (for example, Bruno was sad because he had left his friends behind). Ask children to suggest an alternative word to replace 'sad'.

- Ask: *If you were writing this sentence, would you choose 'sad', or one of the alternatives? Why?* ('Sad' is overused, which lessens its impact; the other words are more specific; they give you a clearer picture of how Bruno felt, which is more interesting.)

- Revise the term 'synonym'. Challenge children, working in pairs, to find as many synonyms as they can for another overused word (such as, 'big') in a given time limit (such as, two minutes).

- Give out the thesauruses. Then write a sentence using the verb 'to go' (for example. Bruno went downstairs). Ask children to rewrite the sentence replacing the word 'went' with a suitable synonym from the thesaurus. Discuss the nuances of meaning in the synonyms children have selected.

- Hand out photocopiable page 24 'Better words' for completion individually or in pairs. (Possible answers: 1. unsightly, 2. delightful, 3. heated, 4. chilly, 5. simple, 6. tricky, 7. briefly, 8. unhurriedly, 9. strange, 10. extremely, 11. influential, 12. task.)

Differentiation

Support: Ask children to answer only half of the twelve questions on the photocopiable page (for example, only odd numbered questions).
Extension: Ask children to choose a short extract from the novel consisting of two or three sentences. Challenge them to rewrite it, replacing as many words as possible with synonyms.

5. Perfect parenthesis

Objective

To use brackets, dashes or commas to indicate parenthesis.

What you need

Copies of *The Boy in the Striped Pyjamas*, interactive activity 'Perfect parenthesis' (Support only)

What to do

- Discuss parenthesis (a technique for adding extra information to a sentence).

- Ask: *Which punctuation marks are used most often for parenthesis?* (brackets) Ask children to look for examples of brackets in the novel and then share their examples. Establish that if you remove the parenthesis, the rest of the sentence still makes sense, for example 'After all, she had never done anything (as far as he knew) other than be his family's maid.' (Chapter 6)

- Bring the children's attention to examples in the novel of dashes used to indicate parenthesis, for example '"Do I look handsome in my ringmaster's costume?" asked Bruno, for that was what he had been wearing for the party that night – the red and black outfit of a circus ringmaster – and he had been very proud of himself in it.' (Chapter 8).

- Show examples from the novel of commas used to indicate parenthesis, for example 'He continued to stroll and whistle and he continued not to look until the reached the window, which, by a stroke of luck, was also low enough for him to be able to see out of.' (Chapter 3)

- Together choose a sentence from the novel. Devise a phrase that could be added to it in parentheses. Rewrite the sentence with the parenthesis inserted. Challenge children to do the same thing independently for three more sentences, using a different punctuation mark each time.

Differentiation

Support: Give children the interactive activity 'Perfect parenthesis' to complete.

6. 'ough' words

Objective

To spell words containing the letter string 'ough'.

What you need

Interactive activity 'Tough rhymes', sticky notes.

What to do

- Organise children into pairs, giving each pair a set of sticky notes.

- Write the letter string 'ough' on the board. Give pairs a set time (such as, two minutes) to write as many words containing the letter string 'ough' as they can; one word on each sticky note.

- Ask each pair to join with another and arrange the words they have written according to the sound the letters 'ough' make in the word.

- Come back together as a class and discuss the different sounds made by the 'ough' letter string. There are seven main sounds: 1. 'ought', 'bought', 'thought', 'nought', 'brought', 'fought' and 'sought'; 2. 'rough', 'tough' and 'enough'; 3. 'though', 'although' and 'dough'; 4. 'plough', 'bough' and 'drought'; 5. 'thorough' and 'borough'; 6. 'cough' and 'trough'; and 7. 'through'.

- Introduce the interactive activity 'Tough rhymes' and give children time to complete the game, playing in pairs to connect each 'ough' word to its rhyming partner.

- End the lesson with a spelling quiz. Read out a sentence containing one of the 'ough' words covered during the lesson, and ask children to write the word.

Differentiation

Extension: Challenge children to i) find a word in which the 'ough' letter string makes the sound 'up' (hiccough); ii) make the longest 'ough' word they can (such as 'thoughtlessness' – 15 letters).

Build a noun phrase

● Write a noun phrase to describe each picture.

1. _____

2. _____

3. _____

4. _____

5. _____

6. _____

7. _____

8. _____

Significant suffixes

> The suffixes 'ant', 'ance' and 'ancy' are used:
> - if there is a related word with a short or long 'a' sound in the right position ('ation' endings are often a clue).
>
> The suffixes 'ent' and 'ence'/'ency' are used:
> - after a soft 'c' sound
> - after a soft 'g' sound
> - after 'qu'
> - if there is a related word with a short 'e' sound in the right position.

- Use the spelling rules above to select the correct spelling of each word in bold in the sentences below.

    1. Lieutenant Kotler worked as an **assistent/assistant** to Bruno's father.

    2. It wasn't clear what had happened to the previous **occupant/occupent** of the house.

    3. The story is told through the **innocent/innocant** eyes of a nine-year-old boy.

    4. Both boys felt **expectent/expectant** about their upcoming adventure.

    5. Shmuel was **intelligent/intelligant** and well educated.

    6. Like all good explorers, Bruno was **observent/observant**.

    7. Bruno made **frequant/frequent** trips to see Shmuel.

    8. Shmuel was grateful to get some **decent/decant** food from Bruno.

- Use four correctly spelled 'ant'/'ent' word from the above task to make a word ending in 'ance'/'ancy' or 'ence'/'ency'. Use the new word in a sentence of your own.

_____

_____

_____

_____

Better words

● Using a thesaurus, select a synonym for each bold word and write it on the line.

1. There was an **ugly** chest of drawers in the bedroom.

   _____

2. The words of the poems Bruno read sounded **beautiful**.

   _____

3. Bruno thought perhaps the people on the other side of the fence didn't have any **hot** water.

   _____

4. There was something about the new house that made Bruno feel **cold**.

   _____

5. It wasn't **easy** to make best friends for life.

   _____

6. Bruno found the words of the poems **hard** to understand.

   _____

7. Father glanced at Bruno and Gretel **quickly**.

   _____

8. Bruno walked **slowly** towards the window.

   _____

9. Bruno thought Shmuel had a **funny** name.

   _____

10. The soldiers were always **very** polite to Father.

   _____

11. Everyone said Bruno's father was an **important** man.

   _____

12. Bruno's father had a special **job** to do.

   _____

PLOT, CHARACTER & SETTING

1. Short and sweet

Objective

To précis longer passages.

What you need

Copies of *The Boy in the Striped Pyjamas*, photocopiable page 29 'Which chapter?', computers (optional), interactive activity 'Précis this!' (support only).

What to do

- Give out copies of *The Boy in the Striped Pyjamas* and photocopiable page 29 'Which chapter?'. Ask children to identify the chapter (Chapter 9), and describe the differences between the précis and the original chapter. (The précis is much shorter, written in the present tense, and contains no dialogue.)

- Work with the class to write a précis of another chapter within a set word limit (such as 100 words). Discuss each stage of the process: skimming the text with the purpose of identifying and noting main events; expanding notes into full sentences; linking sentences; checking for sense; counting the number of words; redrafting; proofreading for spelling and punctuation errors; and producing a final draft.

- On the board write a list of the stages in the précis-writing process: 1. noting, 2. expanding, 3. linking, 4. checking, 5. counting, 6. redrafting and 7. proofreading.

- Challenge children to write a précis of another chapter, referring to the list of stages on the board while working. You may want to let children use a word processing program, as it will streamline the redrafting process.

Differentiation

Support: Ask children to precis the passage from the interactive activity 'Précis this!' instead of précising a whole chapter.
Extension: Challenge children to write a précis of the entire novel within a given word limit (250 words).

2. Significant settings

Objective

To draw inferences.

What you need

Copies of *The Boy in the Striped Pyjamas*.

What to do

- Revise the term 'setting' (where the action in a narrative takes place). Ask children to identify the settings in *The Boy in the Striped Pyjamas*. Establish that there are three principal settings: the house in Berlin, the house at Out-With, and the camp (the other side of the fence).

- Discuss how setting affects the emotions of the characters (for example, Bruno feels happy and relaxed in Berlin but lonely and ill-at-ease at Out-With.)

- Establish that some settings can tell you something about a character, such as Bruno's father's office (described in Chapter 5). Together, read the passage describing the office. Ask: *What can you tell about Bruno's father from the description of his office?*

- Ask pairs to discuss what one of the other character's rooms might be like (for example, Bruno's bedroom in Berlin, or Shmuel's bedroom back home), drawing inferences from what they know about the person's character.

- Challenge children to write a description of Bruno's or Shmuel's room or another setting associated with one of the other characters.

- Ask children to share their written descriptions. They should be prepared to justify what they have written using inference from what they know about the related character.

Differentiation

Support: Provide children with a word bank containing vocabulary that could be used to describe Bruno's or Shmuel's room.
Extension: Challenge children to think of examples from other books they have read in which settings reveal something about character.

PLOT, CHARACTER & SETTING

3. Discovering dialogue

Objective

To identify how language contributes to meaning.

What you need

Copies of *The Boy in the Striped Pyjamas*, photocopiable page 30 'Discovering dialogue'.

What to do

- Discuss how most of the story in *The Boy in the Striped Pyjamas* is told through dialogue between the characters.

- Give out copies of the novel and photocopiable page 30 'Discovering dialogue'.

- Ask children, working individually or in pairs, to choose a section of dialogue between Bruno and another character. You might want to give them a list of passages to choose from (for example, the dialogue between Bruno and Father in Chapter 5, Bruno and Shmuel in Chapter 12, Bruno and Gretel in Chapter 14, or Bruno and Lieutenant Kotler in Chapter 15).

- When children have read their chosen section of dialogue, ask them to complete the photocopiable sheet. The last question asks them to write a few extra lines of dialogue between the same two characters. Challenge children to match the language they use to the language used by the author.

- Bring the class back together. Ask: *What does dialogue add to the story? How might the story be different if there were no dialogue? Would it be as engaging? Why not?*

- Ask selected children to read out the dialogues they have written.

Differentiation

Support: Group less confident children together. They could discuss the questions on the photocopiable sheet without writing the answers, and collaborate to write the extra lines of dialogue.

4. Character profiles

Objective

To infer characters' feelings, thoughts and motives from their actions.

What you need

Copies of *The Boy in the Striped Pyjamas*, photocopiable page 31 'Character profile', sticky notes.

What to do

- Organise children into groups and give out copies of *The Boy in the Striped Pyjamas*. Ask groups to write the names of all the characters in the book. They could write the names on sticky notes.

- Ask groups to rank the characters in order of importance. Encourage group members to collaborate actively, discussing ideas and reaching consensus about character rankings.

- Bring the class back together to compare character lists and rankings. Ask children to justify their reasons for ranking characters in the way they have.

- Ask children to choose a character to complete a character profile for. Give out copies of photocopiable page 31 'Character profile'. The first three questions ask for information that can be found in the text or directly inferred from it. The second three questions ask children to use this information to make more imaginative inferences about the characters.

- Ask children to pair up with a partner who has written a profile of a different character and discuss the similarities and differences between the characters.

Differentiation

Support: Pair children up to discuss the questions on the photocopiable sheet and to complete it together.
Extension: Ask children to write three further inferential character-related questions like the final three questions on the photocopiable sheet. They can swap questions with a partner and answer each other's questions.

5. Changing characters

Objective

To make comparisons within books.

What you need

Copies of *The Boy in the Striped Pyjamas*.

What to do

• Together, read the following passage from the novel: Chapter 3, from 'He ran into Gretel's room…' to '"…You're messing it up."'

• Ask: *What do we learn about Gretel in this passage? How does the author build her character?*

• Establish that authors can build characters by describing what the characters looks like, what they say, what they do, or what they think. Establish that characters often change in some way throughout the course of a story.

• Together, read the following passage: Chapter 16, from 'Gretel's room had changed…' to '"If you make it quick," she said'. Ask: *What do we learn about Gretel in this passage? How does the author build her character? How has Gretel changed since Chapter 3? What do you think may have caused her to change?*

• Ask children, working in pairs, to choose a character from the novel, and to find two passages that reveal that character's personality – one towards the beginning of the novel and one towards the end.

• Ask pairs to discuss how the character is built in each passage, whether and how the character changes, and the possible reasons for any changes.

• Ask selected pairs to share their ideas with the rest of the class.

Differentiation

Support: Give children the page numbers of suitable passages for their chosen character.
Extension: Ask children to track the changes a character undergoes through three passages rather than two.

6. Pondering the plot

Objective

To discuss and identify plot conventions.

What you need

Copies of *The Boy in the Striped Pyjamas*, printable page 'Pondering the plot', interactive activity 'Ordering events'.

What to do

• Display the interactive activity 'Ordering events', asking children to drag the various events from *The Boy in the Striped Pyjamas* into the correct order.

• Ask: *What is the term used to describe the sequence of events in a story?* (the plot)

• Remind children that standard plot structure consists of four phases. Challenge them, working in pairs, to write down these four phases. Depending on their prior knowledge, you may want to give them an out-of-sequence list of plot phases to order.

• Establish the correct order of the plot phases (exposition, conflict, climax, resolution) and ask children to explain each phase. (The exposition introduces the characters and the setting; the conflict introduces one or more problems; the climax is the turning point in the story; and the resolution is the ending.)

• Ask: *Does The Boy in the Striped Pyjamas fit standard plot structure?* Ask children to use the printable page 'Pondering the plot' to summarise the main events in the story and to fit chapters to the phases. (Exposition: Chapters 1–4; Conflict: Chapters 5–17 or 5–18; Climax: Chapters 18–19 or 19; Resolution: Chapter 20)

• Discuss how closely the plot of the book fits standard plot structure.

Differentiation

Extension: Ask children to compare and contrast the plot structure of *The Boy in the Striped Pyjamas* with another story they have read.

7. Thinking about themes

Objective

To identify and discuss themes.

What you need

Copies of *The Boy in the Striped Pyjamas*, printable page 'Thinking about themes', interactive activity 'Identifying themes' (Extension only).

What to do

- Ask: *What is The Boy in the Striped Pyjamas about?* Get children to discuss this question with a partner, and write an answer in no more than 20 words. (for example: The son of the commandant at a concentration camp who makes friends with one of the boys held prisoner there.). Ask the children to repeat the exercise using no more than 10 words (for example: Two boys who make friends across a fence.), and finally, just one word (friendship).

- Explain that these one-word answers reflect what the story is about at the deepest level – its themes. Themes can often be expressed by a single word – usually an abstract noun, such as 'friendship'.

- Using the theme of friendship as an example, ask: *What messages does the author communicate through this theme?* (that friendship can break down the barriers that divide people)

- Organise the class into groups, giving each group a copy of the printable page 'Thinking about themes'. Ask groups to discuss the questions fully before writing their answers.

- Share ideas as a whole class.

Differentiation

Support: Ask children to consider familiar stories, such as fairy tales, and identify their themes, referring to the list of common themes on the printable page.

Extension: Challenge children to complete the interactive activity 'Identifying themes', where they choose the best theme for a passage from the text.

8. Foreshadowing

Objective

To discuss and evaluate how authors use language, considering the impact on the reader.

What you need

Copies of *The Boy in the Striped Pyjamas*.

What to do

- Ask: *How did you feel when you realised what had happened to Bruno at the end of the story? Was it a complete surprise, or had the author given any hints earlier on in the story about what might happen at the end?* (The author gave hints.)

- Explain that the technique of hinting at what is to come later in the story is called foreshadowing. Give an example of foreshadowing; such as from the end of Chapter 16, after Bruno has had his head shaved: 'When he saw himself in the mirror Bruno couldn't help but think how much like Shmuel he looked now…' Ask: *What does this suggest?* (It suggests that Bruno may be able to pass as a prisoner on the other side of the fence, and therefore, that he might go there.)

- Organise children into groups, asking them to find and note other examples of foreshadowing in the novel. Assign a different range of chapters to each group.

- Come back together as a class to discuss the examples of foreshadowing children have found. Establish that the author needn't have used foreshadowing. Ask children to suggest why he might have chosen to do so.

Differentiation

Support: Give children a single chapter to search rather than a range of chapters. Chapters with examples of foreshadowing include 2, 5, 6, 12, 14, 16 and 18.

Which chapter?

- The text below is a précis of one of the chapters in *The Boy in the Striped Pyjamas*.

1. Which chapter is the text below a précis of? _____

> Nothing changes for a while, until Father decides it's time for the children to return to their studies. Their new tutor, Herr Liszt, believes history and geography are the only worthwhile subjects, and refuses to teach things Bruno enjoys, like reading and art.
>
> Bruno becomes curious about what's going on at Out-With. He remembers he used to enjoy exploring back in Berlin, and he realises he could go exploring again.
>
> Despite the fact that his parents have told him repeatedly that exploring is not allowed, Bruno sets off on an expedition along the fence.

2. Compare the précis with the original chapter. How are they different?

_____

_____

_____

_____

_____

_____

_____

_____

_____

_____

_____

Discovering dialogue

● Choose a section of dialogue between Bruno and another character and answer the questions.

The chosen dialogue is on page(s) _____

The person Bruno is talking to is _____

1. What does the dialogue reveal about:

   Bruno?

   _____

   _____

   the other person?

   _____

   _____

   what they think and feel about each other?

   _____

   _____

2. Does the dialogue advance the story? _____

   If so, how?

   _____

   _____

3. Is there humour in the dialogue? _____

   If so, what is the humour based on?

   _____

   _____

4. Write a few extra lines of dialogue between the same two characters.

   _____

   _____

   _____

Character profile

● Write a profile for one of the characters in the book.

Character's name _____

1. What do they look like?

   _____

   _____

2. What are their three main character traits?

   ● _____

   ● _____

   ● _____

3. Which actions reveal these traits? Give one example for each trait.

   ● _____

   ● _____

   ● _____

4. What four things do you think they might have in their bag or pocket?

   ● _____

   ● _____

   ● _____

   ● _____

5. What do you think their most prized possession might be? Why?

   _____

   _____

6. If they were granted three wishes, what do you think they might wish for?

   ● _____

   ● _____

   ● _____

TALK ABOUT IT

1. It happened to me

Objective

To give well-structured descriptions, explanations and narratives.

What you need

Audio recording equipment (Extension only).

What to do

- Ask children to think about Bruno's experiences in the story, identifying those experiences that could happen at any time and in any place. Ask: *Which experiences does Bruno have that any child might have?*

- Give children a few minutes to discuss this question with a partner, before bringing the class back together to share ideas. Children might mention Bruno's experiences of moving home, feeling lonely, not getting on very well with his sister, being picked on, making friends, and going exploring.

- Encourage children to link Bruno's experiences to their own. Ask: *Which of Bruno's experiences do you relate to the most strongly? Why?* Give children a few minutes to discuss this question with a partner.

- Ask children to choose a particular experience from their own lives that relates to Bruno's experience in some way. Tell them they will be telling this story to a group.

- Give children some thinking time to decide which experience they will relate and to think about what they will say.

- Organise children into groups to tell their stories to one another.

Differentiation

Extension: Ask children to create an audio recording of their story to share with another class or to upload to the school learning platform.

2. Stereotypes

Objective

To participate in discussions.

What you need

Copies of *The Boy in the Striped Pyjamas*, photocopiable page 35 'Stereotypes'.

Cross-curricular link

PSHE

What to do

- Ask: *What is a stereotype?* When we stereotype people we don't see them as individuals. Give a few examples of stereotypes (such as the mad scientist).

- Ask children to identify stereotypes in *The Boy in the Striped Pyjamas*: the anxious mother, the strict father, the adventurous boy (Bruno), the flirtatious girl (Gretel) or the clever Jew (Shmuel and Pavel).

- Organise the class into groups, providing each group with a copy of photocopiable page 35 'Stereotypes'. Ask them to discuss the questions on the sheet. All three opening statements are stereotypes, as they present a fixed idea about a group of people. When discussing question 4, it may be worthwhile to discuss what 'positive' means. Does it mean non-derogatory, or leading to positive outcomes?

- Invite each group to report back to the class. Establish that the problem with stereotypes is that they can lead to prejudice (a negative attitude towards a person because of a group they belong to). Prejudice can lead to active discrimination (unfair treatment) and this in turn can lead to persecution (acts of cruelty and brutality).

- Ask children to identify examples of prejudice, discrimination and persecution in the novel.

Differentiation

Support: Ask children to identify stereotypical characters from familiar stories and consider how each character reflects the stereotype.
Extension: Ask children to identify characters from familiar stories that break stereotypes, and consider the effect created.

3. Act it out!

Objective

To participate in role play and improvisation.

What you need

Copies of *The Boy in the Striped Pyjamas*.

What to do

- Ask children to discuss their favourite scenes from *The Boy in the Striped Pyjamas*. Ask: *Which scenes do you think would be the most interesting to act out? Why?*

- Organise the children into groups. Ask each group to choose a scene from the novel and create a 'freeze frame' (like a photograph), communicating what's happening through facial expression and body language. Challenge the rest of the class to identify which scene each group has chosen.

- Invite groups to choose a different scene from the novel and mime it (using movement but no sound, like a silent film). Challenge the rest of the class to identify each scene.

- Ask groups to choose a third scene that doesn't appear in the book (for example, Bruno, Karl, Martin and Daniel 'causing chaos' in the summer holidays, or an incident in Shmuel's family life before they were evicted from their home). Tell children that this time they can use both sound and movement.

- If you have the time, let groups perform their improvised scenes for the class, using simple costumes or props if appropriate.

Differentiation

Support: Help children draw out ideas for what might happen in their improvised scene through asking questions and encouraging discussion.
Extension: Invite children to perform an improvised monologue, role-playing one of the characters, and saying what they really think and feel about a particular event in the story.

4. Dealing with bullying

Objective

To give well-structured descriptions and explanations for different purposes, including for expressing feelings.

What you need

Copies of *The Boy in the Striped Pyjamas*.

Cross-curricular link

PSHE

What to do

- Re-read the passage in Chapter 3 describing Bruno being tormented by one of Gretel's friends, and the passage in Chapter 12 describing Shmuel's treatment by Luka.

- Ask: *What is similar in Bruno's and Shmuel's experiences?* (They've both been bullied.) Ask: *What is bullying?* (deliberately and repeatedly hurting another person) Discuss the various forms bullying can take, including physical and verbal abuse, and the fact that the pain it causes can be physical and/ or emotional. Ask: *How does it feel to be bullied? What other effects can bullying have?*

- Ask: *What advice would you give Bruno and Shmuel to help them deal with the bullying?* Divide the class into groups to discuss this question. Encourage children to come up with (and make a brief note of) as many strategies as they can.

- Come back together as a class to discuss the children's strategies and to add any appropriate advice of your own.

- Make yourself available immediately after the lesson for any children who want to talk to you privately about bullying.

Differentiation

Extension: Ask children to discuss the reasons why some people bully others.

▼ TALK ABOUT IT

5. What do you think?

To articulate and justify answers, arguments and opinions.

Photocopiable page 36 'What do you think?'.

What to do

- Before the lesson, make a large copy of photocopiable page 36 'What do you think?' and cut out the five questions along the dotted lines.

- Share the lesson objective with the class, establishing the meanings of the terms 'articulate' (express clearly) and 'justify' (explain the reasons for your opinions, using evidence from the text).

- Display one of the questions from the photocopiable page. Read it aloud together, ensuring children understand it.

- Give children a short time (between one and three minutes) to think about the question silently, on their own.

- Organise children into pairs and give them time to discuss the question with their partner. Emphasise the importance of turn-taking in the discussion. Remind the child who is not speaking to listen carefully to what their partner has to say, and to ask them follow-up questions.

- Bring the class back together, asking selected pairs to share what they discussed. Encourage children to express themselves clearly and to justify their answers and opinions. When they have finished speaking, encourage listeners to ask questions.

- Repeat the think-pair-share process for more of the questions from the photocopiable sheet, getting children to change partners for each question.

Support: Pair less confident learner with a more confident learner with a supportive and encouraging attitude.
Extension: Challenge children to devise and write questions about the novel for others to discuss.

6. Stand up and speak out!

To participate in presentations.

Photocopiable page 37 'Presentation notes', internet access.

Computing

What to do

- This activity may take more than one session.

- Discuss examples in the novel of characters failing to stand up against injustice (such as no one stepping in to protect Pavel from Kotler).

- Discuss examples of characters standing up and speaking out against injustice (such as Bruno's grandmother denouncing her son for being a Nazi, or Bruno standing up to his father).

- Explain that throughout history there have been people who have stood up and spoken out against injustice. Tell children they will be researching one of them and giving a presentation about them.

- Give children a list of human rights activists to choose from, such as Oskar Schindler, Nelson Mandela, Mahatma Gandhi, Rosa Parks, Shirin Ebadi and Daw Aung San Suu Kyi.

- Give out photocopiable page 37 'Presentation notes'. Ask children to research the answers to the questions for their chosen person, and make notes on what they find out. Discuss effective research techniques, and revise the school guidelines for being safe online.

- Once children have finished writing their notes, discuss performance criteria for an effective presentation, such as ensuring appropriate volume, clarity, pace, intonation and eye contact.

- Ask children to work with a partner to practise their presentation.

- Invite children to give their presentations. Ask the class to assess each presentation in terms of the features they have been considering.

Stereotypes

● Consider the three statements. Then answer the questions below.

1. Which statements do you think are stereotypes? Why?

● Girls talk a lot.

● Teenagers are badly behaved.

● Boys can't sit still.

2. Why do you think stereotypes exist?

3. What problems can stereotypes cause?

4. Can a stereotype be positive? If so, how? / If not, why not?

5. Why do you think the author uses stereotypes in *The Boy in the Striped Pyjamas*?

What do you think?

● Cut out the five questions.

How might the story have been different if it had been written from Shmuel's perspective instead of Bruno's?
Do you think it would have worked as well? Why? / Why not?

'Bruno's father is not a believable character.' Do you agree? Why? / Why not?
Why do you think the author chose to make Bruno's father like this?

If you were Shmuel, would you have forgiven Bruno for betraying you?
Why? / Why not?

Bruno's grandmother says, 'You wear the right outfit and you feel like the person you're pretending to be.'
How is this idea explored in the story?

Bruno's father says, 'Those people…well, they're not people at all, Bruno.'
What is the significance of this statement in the story?

Presentation notes

● Make notes about the human rights activist you have chosen.

Introduction
Who are / were they?
What injustice did / do they stand up to?
Where? When?

Main body
What did they do / have they done to fight injustice?
What problems and dangers did / do they encounter?
If they are no longer alive: How did they die?

Conclusion
What did they achieve? What have they achieved so far?
What do you think about them?

GET WRITING

1. Effective descriptions

To select appropriate grammar and vocabulary to enhance meaning.

Copies of *The Boy in the Striped Pyjamas*.

What to do

- Together, read one or more descriptions of people from *The Boy in the Striped Pyjamas*, such as the description of Lieutenant Kotler from Chapter 7, or the description of Shmuel from Chapter 10.

- After reading each description, ask: *What does the author communicate about the person in this description? How does he communicate it?* Identify and discuss the grammar and vocabulary choices that help the author to do this.

- Ask children to think about a particular person. This might be another character from *The Boy in the Striped Pyjamas*, a character from another book they have read, or a real person they know. Ask children not to choose anyone in school.

- Encourage children to describe the person they want to write about to a partner.

- Challenge children to write a description of their chosen person, selecting grammar and vocabulary to enhance meaning.

- Ask children to pair up with a different partner and read each other their descriptions. Can they guess what their partner is trying to communicate about the person through their description? How successful were they?

Support: Ask children to make their written descriptions very short (for example, two or three sentences). Focus the challenge on the quality of their writing, not the quantity.
Extension: Ask children to find and discuss effective descriptions of people from other books they have read.

2. Film poster

To identify the audience for and purpose of the writing and use other similar writing as models for their own.

Copies of *The Boy in the Striped Pyjamas*, posters for children's films (such as *Hugo, Shrek, Diary of a Wimpy Kid* and *Harry Potter),* film poster of *The Boy in the Striped Pyjamas*.

Art

What to do

- Display posters for recent films around the classroom.

- Organise children into groups, giving each group one set of film posters to focus on. Ask groups to discuss and make a note of the features the film posters share.

- Bringing the class back together, ask children to share their observations.

- Ask: *What is the purpose of a film poster?* (to persuade people to watch the film) *What is the target audience for each poster? How can you tell? What techniques do the film posters use to achieve their purpose?*

- Ask: *Which film poster do you think is most effective? Why?* Get children to discuss this question with a partner.

- Tell children *The Boy in the Striped Pyjamas* has been made into film. Ask whether any of them have seen it, and if so, what they thought of it.

- Ask children to design and make their own film poster for *The Boy in the Striped Pyjamas*, incorporating the features they identified in the group activity.

- After children have finished their posters, show them the real poster for the film. Ask them to compare their own work with the real poster. Ask: *Which poster do you think is more effective? Why?*

3. The Fury

Objective

To note and develop initial ideas, drawing on reading and research where necessary.

What you need

Copies of *The Boy in the Striped Pyjamas,* media resource 'Biographical portraits', photocopiable page 41 'Biography of Mother Teresa', photocopiable page 42 'Biography questions'.

Cross-curricular link

History

What to do

- Note: this lesson may take several sessions.

- Ask: *Who is The Fury?* Establish that The Fury is Adolf Hitler, the head of the Nazi party, and the leader of Germany. Establish that Hitler was a dictator, and discuss the meaning of this term. You could display and discuss the photos of Adolf Hitler from media resource 'Biographical portraits'.

- Ask: *Where do you think Bruno's name for him, The Fury, comes from?* (It is Bruno's attempt to say 'der Führer', which means 'the leader' in German.)

- Together, re-read the pages in Chapter 11 that describe The Fury's appearance and behaviour. Ask: *What can you tell about Adolf Hitler from what the author has written? Do you think The Fury is an appropriate name for him? Explain your thinking.*

- Tell children they will be researching information about Adolf Hitler and writing a biography. Ask: *What is a biography? What sort of information does a biography include?*

- Together, read and discuss photocopiable page 41 'Biography of Mother Teresa', photocopiable page 42 'Biography questions' and look at the photos from media resource 'Biographical portraits'.

- Ask children to research Adolf Hitler's life, and plan and write a biography about him.

Differentiation

Support: Provide a template to help plan a biography and/or a Hitler-related word bank.

4. Missing scenes

Objective

To integrate dialogue to convey character and advance the action.

What you need

Copies of *The Boy in the Striped Pyjamas*, sticky notes in the shape of speech bubbles (Support only).

What to do

- Explain that in a novel an author cannot possibly tell every part of the story in detail; that some parts take place 'off the page' in 'missing scenes'.

- Through paired discussion, ask children to identify places in the book where there might be missing scenes, and, in general terms, what those scenes might be about.

- Invite children to share their ideas with the whole class. Note some of the suggestions on the board.

- Changing discussion partners, ask children to choose one of the missing scenes, and together work out the details of what might happen in it.

- Tell children they are going to write the missing scene they have discussed, basing it around dialogue. Give pairs a few minutes to discuss the following before sharing ideas with the class: *What are the conventions for writing dialogue?* (using inverted commas and starting a new paragraph every time the speaker changes) *What are the characteristics of effective dialogue?* (It uses language people might actually say; it conveys the characters of the speakers, and it advances the action.)

- Ask children to work with their partner to write the missing scene.

Differentiation

Support: Ask children to write dialogue on sticky notes in the shape of speech bubbles. Then challenge them to link the dialogue with narrative.
Extension: Ask pairs to rehearse their missing scene and read it out in front of a group or the whole class.

5. Another ending

Objective

To assess the effectiveness of their own and other's writing.

What you need

Copies of *The Boy in the Striped Pyjamas*.

What to do

- Conduct this activity after children have read the whole novel.

- Ask children to explain how the story ends (events of Chapters 19 and 20). Ask: *How did you feel when you first read the end of the story? Why do you think the author chose to end it this way?*

- Ask: *How else might the story have ended?* Organise the class into pairs and ask children to discuss other possible endings with their partner (for example, instead of Bruno entering through the gap in the fence, Shmuel could have escaped through it, or Bruno's father could have discovered Bruno's clothes in time and intervened to save his son).

- Get children to rewrite the ending of the novel, using one of the ideas they discussed with their partner, or another idea.

- When they have finished writing their endings, invite children to swap work with a different partner, assess the effectiveness of each other's writing, and give one another verbal feedback. Encourage children to revise and refine their endings in the light of the feedback they receive.

- Invite selected children to share their endings with the rest of the class.

Differentiation

Support: Ask children to plan out their ending by writing brief notes, and then use the notes to tell the story verbally to a classmate.

Extension: Encourage children to study the opening pages of the novel and write an alternative first scene.

6. Performing your writing

Objective

To perform own compositions using appropriate intonation and volume.

What you need

Children's writing from activities 3 to 5 in the *Get writing* section, photocopiable page 43 'Checklist for performing your writing', video recording equipment (optional).

What to do

- Remind children of the texts they have written during activities 3 to 5 in the Get writing section (a biography of Adolf Hitler, a missing scene from *The Boy in the Striped Pyjamas* and an alternative ending to the novel).

- Tell children they will be choosing one of these texts to perform in front of an audience.

- Ask children to work in pairs or small groups to brainstorm the characteristics of effective performances.

- Share ideas as a class, and then compare children's ideas with photocopiable page 43 'Checklist for performing your writing'. Give out individual copies of the checklist, asking children to add their own criteria, if appropriate.

- Ask children to choose the piece of writing they want to share, and to practise reading it aloud to a partner. The partner uses a copy of the checklist on the photocopiable sheet to assess their performance. Encourage children to continue practising until their partner is able to tick off every criterion on the checklist.

- Finally, get children to perform their pieces in front of a group, the whole class, or another class.

Differentiation

Extension: Ask children to assess their own performance as well as that of their partner. Children could make video recordings of their rehearsals to facilitate this.

Biography of Mother Teresa

● Read the following text and discuss.

Mother Teresa was a humanitarian. This means she did things to help other people. Her entire life was devoted to helping the poor, the sick, the needy, and the helpless.

Where did Mother Teresa grow up?

Mother Teresa was born in Skopje, Macedonia, on August 26, 1910. Her birth name was Agnes Gonxha Bojaxhiu. She was raised as a Roman Catholic and decided to devote her life to God at a young age.

What did Mother Teresa do?

She joined the Sisters of Loreto at the age of eighteen and started missionary work in Darjeeling, India. When she was thirty-six years old, she felt the call from God to help the poor of India. She had very little support and, while trying to feed the poorest of the poor, she was constantly hungry herself and had to beg for food.

Soon, other women joined her and she formed the Missionaries of Charity. Mother Teresa described their purpose as taking care of 'people who feel unwanted, unloved, uncared for throughout society'. Today the organisation has over 4,000 members who care for people all over the world.

Mother Teresa worked almost up until her death on 5 September 1997.

Interesting facts about Mother Teresa

● In December 2015, Pope Francis recognised a second miracle attributed to Mother Teresa, clearing the way for her to be canonised as Saint Teresa of Calcutta on September 4, 2016.
● She was awarded the Nobel Peace Prize in 1979.
● She once travelled through a war zone to rescue thirty-seven children from the front lines.

Biography questions

Here are some questions to answer in a biography of Adolf Hitler.

- Write three more questions of your own.
- Use your research skills to find out the answers to all the questions. Make notes about what you find out.

Questions	Notes about the answers
What is Adolf Hitler known for?	
When and where was he born?	
What did he do?	
Where and how did he die?	
What effect did he have on the world?	

Checklist for performing your writing

● Use this checklist to assess your partner's performance of their writing.

Performance criteria	Tick when achieved
You speak loudly enough. I can hear you.	
You speak clearly. You do not mumble.	
You speak slowly enough. You do not rush.	
You have good intonation. Your voice goes up and down in the right places.	
You use eye contact. You look at me when you are not looking at the page.	
You use suitable facial expressions.	

ASSESSMENT

1. Drawing inferences

To draw inferences.

What you need

Photocopiable page 47 'Questions, questions…'.

What to do

- Tell the children they are going to answer some questions that will require them to think about the novel *The Boy in the Striped Pyjamas* as a whole.

- Give out copies of photocopiable page 47 'Questions, questions…'. Tell children that as this is an assessment, it is an opportunity to show you what they have understood, so they need to work independently.

- Advise the children to:
  - read all the questions before they attempt to answer any of them
  - start with whichever question they think they will find the easiest to answer; there is no need to attempt the questions in order
  - move onto another question if they get stuck, and come back to the original question later if they have time
  - answer questions as fully as they can.

- Give children a set time in which to answer as many of the questions as they can. When the time is up, take in their work.

- Finally, display a copy of the photocopiable page and discuss the questions and answers together.

Differentiation

Extension: Encourage children to give answers that are as fully developed as possible. If they need more room they can continue their answers on the back of the photocopiable sheet.

2. Discussing opinions

Objective

To participate in discussion about books they have read.

What you need

Copies of *The Boy in the Striped Pyjamas*.

What to do

- Tell children that in this lesson they will have the opportunity to discuss some of their opinions about *The Boy in the Striped Pyjamas* within a group.

- Remind children about your expectations of their behaviour when speaking and listening in a group (for example only one person to speak at a time, listen respectfully, and express your opinion politely). Remind children that it's perfectly alright for there to be differences of opinion within a group, but that it's not alright for them to argue over these differences.

- On the board write some topics for discussion based on personal opinion about the whole book (for example, favourite character; least favourite character; funniest moment; saddest moment; biggest surprise; best chapter). Give groups plenty of time for discussion, so that they can explore several of these topics. Assess individual children's attainment from their contribution to the discussion, drawing out more reticent speakers through questioning where needed.

- Bring the class back together, asking groups to share the most interesting points that came up in their discussion. Encourage children to explain and justify their opinions.

Differentiation

Extension: Ask children to devise and discuss additional opinion-related questions about *The Boy in the Striped Pyjamas*.

3. Unanswered questions

Objective

To ask relevant questions to improve their understanding.

What you need

Copies of *The Boy in the Striped Pyjamas* (optional).

What to do

- Ensure all children have finished reading the novel before you conduct this activity.

- Explain that it's not possible for an author to explain absolutely everything in a novel. Ask children to suggest why this is the case (for example it would complicate the plot too much; it would make the novel too long; it would interrupt the flow; it would be boring).

- Tell children that during this activity they will be identifying some of the unanswered questions in the novel.

- Ask children to give you a list of question words. Write them on the board ('Who', 'Where', 'When', 'Why', 'What', 'Which' and 'How').

- Ask: *What unanswered questions do you have about* The Boy in the Striped Pyjamas? Get children to discuss this in pairs or small groups, and make a note of the questions they have.

- Bring the class back together, asking children to share their unanswered questions. Discuss what the answers might be and why.

- Use the questions asked, as well as the answers given, to assess individual children's understanding of the novel.

4. Book reviews

Objective

To recommend books they have read.

What you need

Media resource 'Book reviews.

What to do

- Tell the children they will be writing a review of *The Boy in the Striped Pyjamas* which they will then share with others (for example, via the school learning platform, the public library, or email correspondence).

- Display and discuss the media resource 'Book reviews'. Ask: *What do these reviews have in common? Who is the intended audience? How do you know? Which book would you most like to read? Why?*

- Ask: *What will you include in your book review of* The Boy in the Striped Pyjamas? Get children discussing this question in groups. Ask groups further questions to help them clarify what they will write: How much of the plot will you give away? Will you use a scoring system? If so, which type? Who will you share your book review with and how will you share it? How will this influence what you write and how you present it?

- Get children to plan, write and revise their book reviews independently. You can then assess each completed book review against the lesson objective. Involve children in the process of distributing their book reviews to the intended audience.

Differentiation

Support: Ask children to base the format of their review on the sample reviews from the media resource 'Book reviews'.

Extension: Challenge children to read one of John Boyne's other novels, and present an oral review to the rest of the class.

5. A letter to the author

Objective

To propose changes to vocabulary, grammar and punctuation to enhance effects and clarify meaning.

What you need

Computers (optional).

What to do

- Ask children to imagine they could talk to John Boyne, the author of *The Boy in the Striped Pyjamas*. Ask: *What would you want to tell him?*

- Get children to discuss these questions in pairs or small groups and then report back to the class. Tell children they will be writing a letter to John Boyne.

- Revise the features of formal letters, including address and date placement, and options for starting and ending the letter.

- Ask children to write the first draft of their letter independently. This stage offers an opportunity for assessing each child's understanding of the novel.

- Assign each child a writing partner. Encourage partners to help each other improve their drafts by honing vocabulary, grammar and punctuation. This stage offers an opportunity to assess individuals against the activity objective.

- Ask children to create a final draft of their letter.

Differentiation

Support: Provide children with a word bank of suitable phrases to include in their letter.

6. Up for debate

Objective

To explain and discuss their understanding of what they have read through formal debate.

What you need

Copies of *The Boy in the Striped Pyjamas*.

What to do

- Provide a controversial motion for a class debate based on *The Boy in the Striped Pyjamas*, such as: If Bruno and Shmuel had met outside Out-With they would not have become friends. Divide the class into two equal teams: one to propose the motion and one to oppose it. It's advisable to allocate children to teams randomly.

- Divide each team into smaller groups in order to prepare their arguments. Encourage communication between groups on the same team to ensure arguments aren't duplicated.

- Choose a moderator to lead the debate. You could do this yourself, or select a child for the role. When all the arguments have been prepared, the moderator introduces the motion, and invites representatives from each team to present their arguments, alternating between the two teams.

- After the prepared arguments have been presented, give teams the opportunity to prepare and present rebuttals in response to the opposing side's arguments.

- Complete the debate by asking children to vote for the point of view that was supported by the most compelling arguments. Assess individuals against how well they participated in the debate.

Differentiation

Extension: During the debate, ask one or two children to keep notes summarising the arguments on each side, and ask them to provide a quick recap before the vote.

Questions, questions…

● Answer these questions as fully as you can.

1. Who do you think is most responsible for Bruno's death? Why?

_____

_____

_____

_____

2. When Bruno is talking to Shmuel, he makes lots of mistakes about what life is like on Shmuel's side of the fence. Why do you think Shmuel doesn't correct him?

_____

_____

_____

_____

3. Why do you think the author decided to tell the story through the eyes of a nine-year-old boy?

_____

_____

_____

_____

4. What do you think is the most important message in *The Boy in the Striped Pyjamas*?

_____

_____

_____

_____

SCHOLASTIC

Available in this series:

978-1407-16066-5

978-1407-16053-5

978-1407-16054-2

978-1407-16055-9

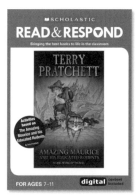

978-1407-16056-6

978-1407-16057-3

978-1407-16058-0

978-1407-16059-7

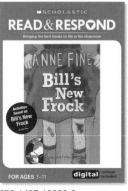

978-1407-16060-3

978-1407-16061-0

978-1407-16062-7

978-1407-16063-4

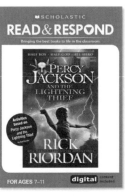

978-1407-16064-1

978-1407-16065-8

978-1407-16052-8

978-1407-16067-2

978-1407-16068-9

978-1407-16069-6

978-1407-16070-2

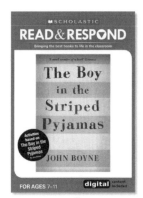

978-1407-16071-9

To find out more, call: 0845 6039091
or visit our website www.scholastic.co.uk/readandrespond